When We Meet at the Horizon

A Poetic Scream

MALAVIKA VIPIN

NOTION PRESS

ISBN: 978-93-5351-333-7

meetatthehorizon@gmail.com

To my mother

To whom I shall remain indebted for the constant support and encouragement

Love you Amma...

Contents

Preface 9

Acknowledgment 11

Prologue 12

1. Hate the melancholy 13

2. Irony of unforgettable dreams 15

3. She 17

4. The midnight hawk at the club 19

5. Away from the galaxy 21

6. I’m in search of Schrodinger’s Cat! 22

7. Fire of love 24

8. Hung up 25

9. The chef 26

10. Confusion 27

11. Waves 29

12. Zephyr..31

13. Pole star: 33

14. Hide 34

15. The orchid of life 36

16. Cinderella 37

17. The arrows of Time 38

18. The hell number...40

19. Death of an Angel..41

20. Adieu to humanity 43

21. Cremation of the peddler…………………… 44

22. Ganges in Mathura 45

23. The wheel of Time...46

24. Calling of Kashi...48

25. Crucifixion 49

26. When we meet at the horizon 51

27. A Poetic Scream 53

Epilogue 57

Bio 58

Preface

Being a debut writer, I strive hard for a deserving stand on the platform of young, modern poets. This book is an attempt towards to make one step closer to that journey.

'When we meet at the horizon' encapsulates the readers into the glory of their emotions, about their hopes and thoughts. The title emphasis the hope of meeting at the horizon. 'At' is appropriate for a static place; the horizon is the outline of the earth or sky at the furthest point one can see and horizon cannot be specific. So the title implies rare case, won't happen at all. That's why it is molded upon the phrase 'at the horizon' deliberately avoiding the phrase 'on the horizon.'

The horizon can be anywhere on the earth or in the space; it can be a sea level horizon or may be the virtual horizon of lovc and hatred. Non-rhyming verses in this book will make, you enjoy the fine transition of time and emotions as the varying shades of the horizon. From the gray shades of depression and grief to the vibrant shades of hope and expectations.

"Beyond the horizon[i]
I'm waiting for your feedback, honey!"

Malavika Vipin

Acknowledgment

I thank my parents and my sister, whose patience and support was instrumental in accomplishing this task.

I wish to express my sincere gratitude towards my honorable great grandparents for the poetic genes.

I thank my friends for their encouragement.

THANK YOU...

Prologue

This road has not been taken by me
The road itself has taken me to drive this path
Experience leads me through this
The wisdom shelves the blockages
Fuel of enthusiasm eases my journey
I crossed the path with at most happiness
Mist of eagerness sometimes hinders the path
But the love and grace of elders thrive on me
With pleasure I made the stones struck
In my path into beautiful words
'When we meet at the horizon'
A poetic scream, a part of my destiny
Glimpse it without prejudice...

1. Hate the melancholy

Hate the melancholy

But it went as chorus, now.

What if all these noises end?

Eternal peace!

Will it happen?

Even the lord and saints couldn’t accomplish it.

Is there any new avatar to fulfil this?

Err... A big no! No!

From the epic to today’s newspaper

Depict the portrayal of sorrows and miseries.

Eccentric; unending mourning of the world

Optimism lags the flow

And got stuck in the thorns and stones

Smog of revenge and hatred spreads in the world

Its reward overshoot the life as Violence!

The sparks of violence trigger the destruction

War! War! War!

Sprout the seed of peace

Let it blossom happiness in abundance

And shower your soul with love

Enjoy the beauty of the world

Fill the boundaries with brotherhood

End the war! Spread the peace[1]!

---

[1] ***SALUTE TO OUR SOLDIERS: JAI HIND!***

2. Irony of unforgettable dreams

Irony of unforgettable dreams

My dreams, loss its frequency

When the eyes closed

I could only sense the darkness

Are they left me, alone?

Idle in the wheel of existence

The path of reality has narrowed

Submerged in the blank pages

Of life, few chapters left uncovered

Hurdles in the queue of thoughts

Suppressed mind yells for the survival

Not worthy, leave it behind

Even the dreams itself can't fly.

Like the rhymes in the free verse

They left behind with no regret

Enjoy the beauty of nonexistence,

An irony of unforgettable dreams!

3. She

In the mirror, she saw her reflection
But didn't understand herself on it
At that point of life, she herself was a mere
Shadow of her, just a shadow...

Step forth into the world of darkness
But that darkness was insufficient to hold her
Touch of dampness kills its purity
Even the black was not pure enough...

Shades of black filled the void of soul
And the world seems as the remnants of ashes
The ashes of dreams and hope
Flatters through the air and suffocates her...

Oh! Nothing wrong with her
But the truth fired her mind
With the spark of reality
Which pop up vivid emotions

She waits to catch the dawn
The rays of renewed hope and wisdom
With the potential to seal
The womanhood with positivity

To revive her back
From the atrocities and conflicts
From body shaming and fear
From molestation and gang rape

To break the chain
And to live freely
With the glory of humanity
With the power of womanhood

4. The midnight hawk at the club

The midnight hawk at the club,
High-profile attitudes
And the show off money
Beneath the regular scenes,
Is there any new couch?
Any new flavors of vodka?

Dance in the fluorescent lights,
With the beat of music
Oh! Sometimes lose my rhythm,
The drum beats hit my head
Just do it for your sake, to pretend
To believe as a part of civilized society,
And not an introvert, you are.

It kills! But often helps to thrive,

From the loneliness; a minuscule escape

From the baggage of life.

5. Away from the galaxy

Away from the galaxy

I found a home

With the abundance of peace and love

The weather of happiness

And the shades of day merged with joy

I felt the ultimate bliss there

The ocean of success,

We can easily dive into it

Never heard the harsh words

Instead, enjoy the music of tenderness

Tasted the Milky Way

On the way back to earth,

The elixir of love; I felt special

6. I'm in search of Schrodinger's Cat!

Schrodinger's Cat[2]! A mysterious one

Bit of poison in a box and he sealed the cat

Is it dead or alive?

Nobody knows, ridiculous!

Why is his cat a complex Felix[3]?

Is it Pat Sullivan's cat?

The Cat with Australian phonetics

Or Rudyard Kipling's cat?

'The Cat that Walked by Himself[4]'.

I know Minna's cat is cool

Double colored eyes,

---

[2] *It is a paradox, devised by Austrian Physicist Erwin Schrodinger. About quantum superposition.*

[3] *Felix the cat is a cartoon character created by Pat Sullivan in 1919*

[4] *The title of a short story by Rudyard Kipling.*

Simple and playful

Wander here and there

Lovely cat! Minna's cat is Lovey...

Does Schrodinger's cat hunt small prey?

Will they stalk, capture and kill prey?

Is Schrodinger's cat a male or female?

Can it hear vivid frequencies?

Is it a cat without a tail?

Or is it a venomous cat?

Why did Schrodinger try to kill his cat?

Is he an Ailurophobe person?

Is the cat still alive or dead?

I'm in search of Schrodinger's Cat!

7. Fire of love

Blazed fire from his anger

Kills me, it was the anger of love

Waves of vehemence hold the path

Revelation fleets the moment,

Hack the hope and arouses the temperament.

The pain conceals, beneath my soul

It hurts! I lose! I die!

Suffocates him with the flare of hot ashes

The ashes of grief and hatred

But he still loves me

The fire of his love, never ends…

The fire of love, The Life!

8. Hung up

Those irritating bells, beep! Beep!

Nothing persists with the lost relationship,

The lost spark of wishful life

The awkward conversation starts; hello

Not to swirl around

The dank mist of hatred;

The wire winds my neck

Suffocate enough to utter a word

Hung up. I can't.

That voice still drapes me,

Into vicious glory of love.

9. The chef

Toffee pudding in the witching hour

Spawns up a new flavor

The real question mark over the testament

Is the recipe awesome or the chef?

Amour the situation, with no hesitation

Give the compliment; splendid!

But as soon there spread the aroma of romance

Is the pudding awesome or the chef?

Breezy night with languor talks

But dare to make out the hot recipe

It won't work, had tasted once, it ruins the gut

Not anymore, even if the chef is handsome.

10. Confusion

Fascinated by the beauty of the night
Oh! The symphony of silence;
In the splashes of moonlight
Reels the nostalgia
Eyes pretend to be the camera
Capture everything,
Mind obviously the editor
Make the dull night, colorful.

Nostalgia soon spread into the realm of reality,
There arrives the confusions and conflicts...
Soon open the new world; illusion!
New world of illusions twinkle up in the mind
Where to stand? Where to go?
What is the truth? Confusion! Dire confusion!
Winds of change lash her mind;
What to trust and why?

Apart from the soul everything

Dwells in the fairyland

Land of falsehood;

Where life itself is a mystery

Beyond the threshold

Seems the world itself as a shattered illusion

Confusion! Confusion!

11. Waves

Waves! Waves!

Still haunt me

It wasn't blue; I felt everything as gray

Even the magnificent sunset

Crimson sky... Everything seemed to be colorless

I was like the soap bubbles

Over there... Perfect spheres,

With glares of vibrant colors inside

But does anyone notice the inner shades?

Within a tiny span of time, bubble burst up

Everything seems useless...

For some, that was a splendid evening

They shared their friendship

Like couples, she licked his ice cream,

With immense pleasure

Without hesitation, he quaffs it.

Perception is distinct
But sometimes perception might be
Persecution of others
Waves distracted the thoughts

I felt the darkness of night
Whirl around my soul
Even in the glittering lights of the beach,
Everything seems artificial...

12. Zephyr

Where the sun kisses the waves,
I will be there waiting for you.
When the arrows of time trespasses
Your heart, I will be there beside you,
As a Zephyr forever.
Feel my perpetual love,
Beyond the Heavens,
I love you...

When the moon kisses the star,
I will be looking for you.
When the arrows of time breaks,
When the memory vanishes,
My soul weeps for you,
Accept my love.

From the heaven,

Forever as a Zephyr for you…

13. Pole star:
The harbinger of night

The goddess of north rises,
With the nodes of peace and harmony
Blinks the right path and captivates
The soul from darkness
Bright enough to sense the pain
And soothes every heart with tenderness
Close enough as a good companion;
A real insomniac
The harbinger of night...

As I ruffle through the darkest part of life
Will you be my companion?

14. Hide

Hide in the cave

No one will see

Away from the dust

The noxious dust of blame

Away from the pointing fingers

The frostbitten fingers of criticism

Hide on the tree top

No one will catch

Away from the disturbances

The violent disturbances of life

Away from the unnecessary talk

The foolish talk of betrayal

Hide from everything
No one cares

But, dear, how long will you hide?
Away from bizarre life
Away from surreal circumstances
How long? How far?

Don't hide from yourself
There is no way away from you.

15. The orchid of life

In the orchid of life

Love chases you like

A hummingbird.

Tastes the nectar

Loots all your hymns

And fly away.

Wait longer, Stand still

Neglects all the breeze,

Gaze for the long gone sweet heart.

16. Cinderella

Happiness dwindles the desire of her
The desire of oneness, not to be apart...

The hidden fairies of imagination
Pat her shoulder, the wisdom of color
The shades of beauty, mesmerizes her
Every now and then...

In the heaves of flowers
There begins the story of another Cinderella
With the wistful glow of sunrise
The real beauty of innocence reemerge.

17. The arrows of Time

Again the agony happens
Arrows of time pierce my heart,
Struck hard and oozes out my hope
Again, why the past is so much
Blend with the present?
Arrows swift me in the infinite of memories;
Some faces, incidents, dialogues...
It wraps me under the swirl of emotions
And tickles me with the hardships,
Catastrophic flame of wickedness
Still exhaust me with the extreme foul smell
Though it tells the story of pain and misery
The drops of tears were with the essence of love
Let me, exit from this…
And break these arrows to steadfast my life,

To delve into the legacy of love.

To enjoy the ultimate bliss.[5]

[5] *This poem has been selected by the INTERNATIONAL POETRY DIGEST Monthly-The Writer's Network.*

18. The hell number

Thirteen the hell number

Universal number of the devil

Hey, the pleasant one in it... One! 1!

You are still alive right.

What about three?

Three too… is alive

Uh! Then thirteen?

Of course lucky

A few marriages, few birthdays, few visits

Few accommodations...

The daunting list is brief.

The luckiest number!

But the unlucky one

Uh! They trap you in the baggage of witchcraft.

A superstitious myth of an odd day

Wish happily thirteen aloud;

Uh! Without hidden fright.

19. Death of an Angel

Baby, I first saw you

With the glorious charm on your face

The pale red face with a cute smile

My little angel!

My child, I never thought

I would rebirth in this earth

All the pain relinquishes

Saw the blissful future of mine.

Baby you set out my soul from the darkness,

My heart rejoices with the warmth of your presence

But it never lasts more, destiny plays his cruel role

You got called back from the heaven.

Baby I last saw you,

With the glorious charm on your face

The yellow face with a tear drop

Oh, my little angel!

20. Adieu to humanity

Ludicrous treatment, a dreadful insight

Is it a sinful past or curse indeed?

The reckless time, sometimes shows

The beats of heartbeats went through

Intend to sense the parody of one's own self

It anticipates the path of betrayal

Wreck the pulse; anyway, battle curtails

The temperament, though, indulges the ruthless

Agony of mind being the Yew of disturbances

Until the end as a dweeb beast

When the pervasiveness re-codify the strengths

Hurray to the wind not yet bash

Adieu to the humanity, claps! Claps!

21. Cremation of the peddler

Cremation of the peddler
No screams yet...
Solace to an immemorial human
With no definite path, with no mission
He completed his journey.

In the grass veil, he burns
Away from the burbs
To curate the mastery of lies
No one was there.

Innocuous challenge slithers the situation
As soon another peddler takes charge

Exact with no prestige, with no money
To loot the city, but not like the old peddler.

22. Ganges in Mathura

No one notices the splashes
Of Ganges ever in Mathura
It wasn't the drops of the Milky Way
Straight from the heaven
Not the elixir of peace and solace
The riverine flow of pain from the Vrindavan
The tale of longing; O, Krishna be mine...

The Ganges flourished in the mind of Krishna
Overflowed with the illusion of being one
Not apart from each other, satisfied through
The spiritual oneness, beyond the serenity
Of the world, they wrote the saga of true love
The sorrow of Radha and Lord Krishna
A poignant memoir of their life

23. The wheel of Time

Oh, the wheel of time
Now struck at the Kaliyuga
The Yuga of evil and sin
Shades of misery and agony
Filled the mother Earth

Time for yet another avatar
Oh, this time the king of Shambhala
Born as the son of Sumati and Vishnuyasha
Riding a white horse with a sword
Yet another myth... A holy myth
Glorifies the power of Lord Maha Vishnu
Karmic depiction of God, The Kalki
Om Kalki Om is the prayer, is it?

Oh! The descent of the divine
Are you the destroyer of filth?

With enormous power to end the darkness

To destroy the evil and ignorance

Time changes, wheel keeps on rotating

Next the period of Satya Yuga

The Yuga of truth and peace

But the hero? Om Hari Om!

24. Calling of Kashi

Billowed by the thoughts of Kashi

Not yet, in the bris of devotion

The spiritual vengeance of the soul

Not towards the ideal of temple

But towards oneself, to explore

The truth, as a part of universe

And at last to know the supreme

Truth of oneness...

You and me, are the same

We are the universe

Aham Brahmasmi[6]!

A blissful journey to attain Moksha

Om Namah Shivaya!

---

[6] *It is a Sanskrit aphorism meaning I am Brahman. This mahavakya is in the Brihadaranyaka Upanishad.*

25. Crucifixion

When the act of the false self,
Burns up the turmoil of life
Betrayed the own self, burrs the future
Behold the soul to ford
The witty streams of the world
Beneath the wisdom,
The burden of reluctances will emerge
To live with ecstasy,
You will suck the blood of the enemy
Pretend to be dear, wearing the sheep's wool
The real cruel devil with the cunning mind
But when the lantern itself lost in vain
The darkness will encapsulate you
In the deepest void when you meet your true self,
There begins the apocalypse…
The mental irony of self-destruction

Snatches you every night

Ends up in self-crucifixion.

26. When we meet at the horizon

Sun will gaze more, witnessing the catastrophe,
Ever happened in the world. No doubt.
Will the earth holds the flame of our hatred?
Who knows?

Never lame to hide, words sometimes shatters,
The unbidden feelings, maybe not.
But your eyes will speak, for sure,
The ode of demagoguery, which no one can sing.

As the storm of my envies slams upon you,
The enigma of distress will begin,
Ecstasy of pain quills the tale of our wounds
And we once again say goodbye…

So, when we meet at the horizon[ii],

Wave your hands with no hesitation.

As a real stranger, stay away,

Apart! We trample the horizon.

27. A Poetic Scream

When illusion diverts the hurricanes of thought
I started jotting down the words for you
Brew the mist of emotions,
And endure the pain.

Scream! A poetic stream!

Under the blanket of moody sky
I once again ended up with worries,
Somewhere on the street, I miss
The rhythm of peace.
As I walk closer to the enclaves
Of the hidden cocoon,
Noises dampen away...
When the parade of streetlights ends

I saw my shadows, leaving me
Once again alone! No hesitation,
I walk farther
How long? How far?
Beneath the misery
Is there any Cloud Nine?
Oh! This overload kills me
Revoked the anxiety and depression
A zephyr of doubt cuddles my heart
Lurked the midst of frustration
And with the burst of misery
It triggers the gambling of emotions,
That too in the world of betrayals.
Emphasis for the harmony
Burn the turmoil forever
Grave its darkness
Curtail all the uncertainties
Evoked the self-control

Scream! A poetic scream!

Strong enough! Now I can,

Unify the forces of serenity and calmness

I crushed the unwanted voids,

In the midst of illusion

I turnstile the mind ahead

And challenged the deep-rooted fear

All the thoughts whirl around my soul;

Like the sparkling butterflies

They began to fly

With the glittering glow of love and wisdom

Soon the flame of happiness arrives

And scream mutes.

What about the poetic scream?

A poetic scream!

………………………….∞…………………….....

As the arrows of time trespasses, your heart

Your longing, for me, deepens

Hoping to meet ***on the horizon***[iii]*...*

Epilogue

Now don't cast a spell on my book

Dazzling display of words

With devastating emotions

O! Dear, don't miss this ecstasy

Let it resurrect in front of you

A riveting thriller of hard-core vibes

Hope you don't **MIND IT!**

Bio

Malavika Vipin is an insightful Indian writer, native of God's own country, Kerala, Co-author of the anthology ‘Audacity of the blank pages: Writerstolli'. She is an enthusiastic Virgoian with many talents. Rashtrapati Guide (Bharat Scouts and Guide). Her mission is to empower the world with education to build humanity and love.

Daughter of Thekkedath Vipin and Bindu Vipin, (Proprietor: Indobiocoal industries, Kerala, tackle the problems in the fuel sector with biomass energy production). Blessed with a sister Mrudula Vipin, her motivator. Being an empathetic person, help her lot in writing.

meetatthehorizon@gmail.com

https://hellopoetry.com/u727093/

[i] *Beyond the horizon: farther than the possible limit of sight*

[ii] *At the horizon: a specific location, but not exist actually. 'At' is appropriate for a static place; the horizon is the outline of the earth or sky at the furthest point one can see and it cannot be specific. So 'When we meet at the horizon' implies rare case, won't happen at all.*

[iii] *On the horizon :imminent*